Samara's
Beauty and Tussle
By Saraswathi

Published by Saraswathi

Published in 2022

Cover by Saraswathi.

Disclaimer

This story is based on real life experiences. Any resemblance to actual persons living or dead, business, companies, events or locales may be purely coincidental.

<u>Beauty and Tussle</u>

Fate is karma

 Luck is your comfort zone – depends on your effort and bless.

"Every birth Has a purpose".

Story of a girl. Her beauty, knowledge, sacrifices and dedication, And supernatural power". Who enjoyed her All part of life by accepting that, there is a pay back and there is a will and her hope gave her everything.

It was a beautiful city, with powerful temple of goddess, Surrounded by many, Priests and families.

Apart from that, there were many families. Belonging to different categories. But in some areas, completely surrounded by a single caste people, relatives and their families.

It was a beautiful morning in the city. Normally in South India, people wake up early in the morning. They clean and mop the house. In front of the house They sweep and sprinkle cow dung water, draw design called Rangoli and they color it and decorate with Flowers. After, all the members of the family sit together for a morning coffee.

After their bath. They offer their prayers to their God. By lighting a lamp and insense sticks, dhoop to their respective gods and ancestors. Not everyone, in some family, head of the family will.. only do regularly, along with Tulsi Puja and Surya Namaskar, this is a routine. It's Granny she is punctual, her role is important in all families.

It was a beautiful morning. Members of the family, gathered for their breakfast. Granny - son and daughter in law and pregnant daughter, all enjoyed their breakfast.

After breakfast, son left for his office, Granny was sitting on an old wooden chair, daughter in law went to neighbor's home and daughter went to bring water from well (in olden days there were no water taps, people used to bring water from river, lake or well). She brought the water and sat on the floor. She felt discomfort, she told her mother she is getting pain. Yes!, She is yet to give birth to a baby. In those days doctors were not available everywhere. But there will be expert people / nurse who gained knowledge with experience. Granny made her daughter to lie on her bed, she went to neighbor's home told them to inform her son that his sister got delivery pain, meanwhile granny went to another neighbors home and sent him to bring the nurse. As there was no telephone or a car at home, people use cycle to reach others.

As I told, it was a pleasant morning sunrise were falling on trees, flowers, entering the home through windows and doors, but a pregnant women in room covered by lamps and light screens.

We believe that human life is god's wonderful creation and bless, we believe that pregnant women will be blessed by Angels and ancestors.

Pregnant lady was crying with pain, her brother and nurse came many of the neighbor's and relatives gathered and all together sat in the hall. Nurse told the pregnant lady's brother to wait outside the room. She was arranging things like, cloth, hot water, scissor and other required things.

By holding the pregnant lady's hand nurse told her, "Calm down you will be giving birth to an Angel!, you have to tolerate the pain".

Yes, Angel will take birth only if birth is blessed. Yes!, where there is positive energy angels live there, where there is a regular Puja, ancestors will be happy and make the family members feel their presence that they are with them. Angels will be happy with the fragrance of the incense sticks and lamps.

There was a small discussion between the angels, "Baby's eyes will look like my eyes, it will be green". Other one said, "No it will be like mine, it will be brown, another one said "It will be gray and hair will be brown copper color, skin will be pinkish".

 On the other side the ancestors, "See how much pain she is bearing", replying to this the other one said, "Yes, when I gave birth to you, I was also crying and controlling my pain". There was a argument between the ancestors, "She is going to give birth to a baby boy" while the other one said, "No way, she will give birth to a baby girl and she will look like me", another Ancestor said "No, She is a very special birth, who possess lots of knowledge and luck". Suddenly the another ancestor says, "Sorry for interruption, this baby girl will struggle lot in her life, by the people surrounded by her" Everyone was shocked and asked "Why?" The Female ancestor replied that "Its her **Attractiveness**, her **Knowledge** and **Fate** make other jealous".

All were sad, ohh no,,, by hearing this, one asked, "Is there any way to stop or change the fate". Ancestor 3 replied, "No, she is blessed by **God**, life makes her strong and she accept all difficulties and things will be alright, she will enjoy the life along with the troubles from her own blood". One ancestor asked "How sure are you are, that you are telling right?". "Let us see" ancestor 3 replied.

The pregnant lady was crying, 2-3 Ladies were holding her hand and telling her "It's alright, be calm, you are giving birth to beautiful angel".

She delivered and gave birth to a baby girl. Nurse cleaned the baby with hot water and cloth and others cleaned the place, the nurse took the baby outside the room and showed it to granny. Brother was very happy and many others were curious to see the baby. Granny was very happy, all her neighbors are rushing, telling that the she(Baby) looks different. After some time, the nurse took the baby inside the room.

By evening, Granny's son-in-law(Daughter's husband) arrived. He was curious to see the baby, everyone greets him. He entered the room and was very happy and he said "Look at her eyes, skin, color and hair, she is different, special and sweet. Her name should be honey, "I will keep her name Honey" he said to his wife, he took the baby outside the room and sat next to Brother-in-law(Wife's Brother) and baby's father said, "Her name will be **honey",** Brother-in-law said "No it's not possible, we have already decided her name and it will be **Samara,** it means **Smart** and **Beautiful".** Argument went long and it was the beginning of mismatching of opinions between two different minds.

However, there should be an end, Granny took the baby and said it might be hungry, I will ask her mother to feed. Daughter-in-law brought some sweet and distributed it among the family members followed by a delicious dinner.

Days gone, finally it was a naming ceremony day, Astrologer said "In her horoscope 50% of her life she will struggle and 50% of her life she will enjoy, she will succeed. Life will teach her lessons leaps and downs making her strong Her dedication and effort will give everything she lost from her own people and people who cares and love her will be more happy and those who hurts and degrades her will suffer in life". Granny asked "Why and what exactly is there in her horoscope, please detail it", Son also asked, "Is there any Shanthi that we have to do?", Brother-in-law (Sister's husband) argued, "I don't believe this". Astrologer said, "Yes, Unless you experience, you will not trust and some times situations force you to trust and you will find the way to get rid of all your problems".

Finally, naming ceremony started angles and ancestors blessed the baby and the arguments ended between the family members by keeping the baby's name as **"Samara"**, named by Granny and selected by her son, but it was not accepted by the Baby's father and it is the beginning of crack.

Granny in the home takes care of the baby, she plays a major role in baby's life. Months passed and one fine day, Husband(son-in-law) came to take his wife and baby to his home, Granny and her son asked him to let his wife and baby be here for some more days but Son-in-law refused for their request and said that he has an appointment, he has to travel too far from his native, before that he need to spend some time with his daughter. After long discussion, Granny packed daughter and baby's belongings and other required medicine. They set to go, Daughter and Son-in-law left the place.

Parents along with their 3 month old baby, arrived to their native home. People were eagerly waiting to receive them, they received husband wife and the baby with some rituals.

 Sisters and brother(Husband's brothers and sisters) were excited to see the baby, they greet the baby's mother, gave sweet to her and distributed the sweet to gathered members of the family, everything was going good.

On the other side, Granny's daughter-in-law (Son's wife) gave birth to a baby girl. Years gone and the family grown big. Granny's son had 2 Daughters and 1 son, on the other side, Granny's daughter had 2 Daughters and 1 son.

 In olden days, getting a job in any company was not so easy. More over people were working in their own farm land, they grow required grains and vegetables for their home. Even if they are wiling to earn money, they have to work in shop or in the company, it was the beginning of civilization. Far away there were some companies, not for higher positions but for supporting jobs like attender, security and maintenance. Company use to hire known people only with some connection. Granny's son-in-law got a proposal to work as a guard to the company, he said that the quarters will be provided by company, he will be moving soon with his wife and children, everyone were happy.

Family were leading a good life along with other families in the colony. It was a beautiful and well organized place, with open park, children's play area and some stone benches and walking track where people can walk. Breath fresh air and enjoy the nature, whole atmosphere is very pleasant, Samara was admitted to kindergarten school.

Years gone, family decided to visit their native place, Samara's father took his family to his native. He brought some clothes, artificial, ornaments, some sweets for his parents. Brothers and sisters, everyone were happy, Samara's parents spent some time there and decided to visit Granny's home.

By seeing the grand daughter, Granny and her son were more happy, Samara's short dress and Bobcut, she is now going to convent. Grannies eyes were bursting tears in happiness, seeing her little Grand daughter, Granny prepared food and fed it to Samara. All others shared their experience and life in their city and all were happy, they spent some time together.

Everything was good. Some portion of Samara's father's earning was sent to his parents via money order.

 On the other side, in Samara's father's home there were small disputes between her parents and between her father's brothers, sisters and other family members.

They used to grow grains and vegetables, they used bullock to cultivate land for agriculture and they were getting dairy items like milk and curd from cow, but other essentials they have to purchase in shop by exchanging the grains, vegetables and dairy items. As family and children grow up, family will be having some mismatches, in opinion.   Some become jealous, unnecessary arguments, which force to do bad to their own blood.

One day, Postman arrived and stood in front of the gate calling the name of the receiver of the post. Elder sister of Samara's father came and collected the money order and went inside.

Samara's father's parents were happy they told their elder son that they are proud that their son is sending some money.

Now jealousy begins, elder sister and brother of Samara's father become angry, off course all share money received, but when people are not having extra source of income and some one else is earning money. People won't plan to earn by themselves, instead they become greedy and selfish, it makes them to do foolish things which spoils the whole family and creates differences between them.

Each time they receive money, there will be a fight between the family members.

Hey guys, you must remember this line, **"If you can't help someone, no issue. But never try to spoil the happiness of anyone"**. Many might have heard about "Tantra"(A kind of magic which is used for both good and bad) where people use this technique to control people and make them act according to their wish. It was not one, but both elder sister and elder brother did **"Tantra"** to Samara's father. On the same time Elder sister wrote a letter to Samara's father, stating that, parents are sick, come immediately.

Yes! It happened as planned, he arrived and all of them including the parents too acted as if they were sick and did their drama. Finally, Samara's father agreed to come back home with family. He went to his home and shared everything wit his wife, he informed the office that he is resigning from his job, he packed everything and reached his parents home. Everything was good for some time as he had little savings, he spent it. But money is more important in life. He was jobless, he was in discomfort, day by day it makes life unhappy and complicated.

Samara's father-in-law (mother's brother) visited their home there were many members in the family, but sister was doing some work and was busy. Samara's father was not there, others were chit chatting. 'He stood' and waited till evening, By evening, Samara's father came. Samara's father-in-law asked Samara's father to come to his home. Then Husband, wife and their children decided to visit.

Next day in Samara's Granny home, Granny was asking her daughter that how is life, what her husband is doing, how are other members of the family and are you happy?. Granny received a reply that nothing is good, her husband is jobless, no source of income, she is not happy.

Granny shared the same with her son, both granny and her son advised Samara's father to rejoin the same company. But he was not at all ready to hear, all he wanted was to be with his parents and family. Samara's father told his wife to "Get ready we are going to our home". Granny in requesting manner, "What's so hurry, please stay for some more days" . He replied "No, I have some other work and I can't stay. Granny asked Samara's father to leave Samara with her, after once he is settled, he can take her with him. After a long discussion, he agreed and left her with Granny.

In his native, family grown big, all are looking for extra income and some started working, Samara's father's parents had fallen sick.

Somehow Samara's father started **Mess(A Small restaurant).** Where they can earn money to survive. Everything was going good, somehow they all were happy.

"We are Indians, we believe in God, we know there is one supreme power and we all do prayers".

We start our prayers by and with varieties of flowers and varieties of dishes. We chant, do bhajan and also we put our requisition in front of God.

Visiting temple, Chanting, Prayer and bhajans are Samara's best part of her life. Granny is her God mother. Granny and her prayer is only for Samara. Granny's truth, cleanliness and advise was like shadow. Its always protecting Samara. Granny created strength in Samara, Granny was Samara's mother, master and her soul.

"Good practice makes people organized and organized people are always more dedicated in life. Finding mistakes in others will bring unnecessary arguments. Correcting our self and limiting ourselves is always better". This is what Samara learnt in her life.

There are many places where you feel better and experience positive energy. It always depends on how we were brought up.

Samara used to visit temple along with her Granny and Granny's friends. Granny used to circumambulate to all the idols in the temple. In front of all God idols inside the temple. Granny repeatedly pray God to bless Samara with good education and with good health and wealth and family.

In the area which Samara used to stay with her Granny, had many relatives near by, but Samara was younger in the whole street. Granny sometimes let Samara to play with other children for some time, she used to watch Samara playing joyfully with other children. After the play time, if anyone touches, Granny used to bath Samara, change the dress.

Time was melting, everyone were growing. Samara's father-in-law(Granny's Son) used to care Samara much more than his children.

Under the shelter of her father-in-law, Samara completed her graduation. Maturity is the age where person can talk and behave wise.

Everyone in life have one beautiful love story. Sometimes it is one side and sometimes it is triangle. Many love story will be successful love story, but in some cases, break-up, fight, death and will ends with bad memories.

Its Samara's childhood friend, handsome, smart and anger. He started liking Samara, not actually from her childhood but after her graduation. In Samara's college days, Samara's best friends are book and pen, she use right small poem and quotes. Many of Samara's college mates proposed Samara, expressed their love. She was not at all interested in anyone.

Its Samara's childhood friend, Samara's friends were liking him but Samara was not at all worried or advised anybody to not to fall in love.

After Samara's graduation. Samara started her part-time job in a small office. Samara's beauty and nature was attracted by the people who were coming to her office. Her childhood friend was also one among them. Months gone.

One beautiful morning Samara was sitting in her office, her childhood friend came and proposed Samara, he expressed that He loves Samara. Same time Samara's father-in-law came to meet her in her office. By seeing Samara's Father-in-law, Samara's childhood friend left the place. Samara's father-in-law don't like him from the very beginning. Samara's father-in-law advised Samara to not to talk with him and never trust his words. Samara's Father-in-law narrating, "He does not belong to our caste, not much educated, not earning any income, don't have respect for elders and very rude too. Samara replied her father-in-law, "Sorry father-in-law, I don't have any interest in anyone and coming to my marriage, I trust you more than anyone, I know, you have given me everything in my life, whomever you bring as a groom without any second thought I will marry him".

Samara was seeking a full-time job. God sent someone to help her. Many times we attempt and we won't get good opportunity. Sometime by luck, fate introduces people, when we are on our path. Yes!, someone recommended Samara for a good organization.

At home, it was morning time after prayer, Granny blessed Samara. Father-in-law took Samara to the interview. Samara was selected for office Admin work, She had been asked to report to the office from the next day with dress code.

Next day morning, for the first time, Samara wore a Saree. She took Granny and Father-in-law's blessings and reported to the new office. After a month, she received her first salary, she came and gave it to Granny. Granny while directing, "Give this to your Father-in-law" and Father-in-law told to Samara, "You keep this with you". Granny was so happy and she prepared some sweets.

After some time, one morning, Samara received telephone call from her mother. Over the phone Samara's mother was telling, "Your sister needs some money for her studies". The amount was three times more than Samara's salary.

In life, unless we face worst situation, we cannot be careful in making decisions. Knowingly, we accept risk, every small problems will grow big. One worst decision, which was the beginning of all the problems.

Samara promised her mother that she will arrange the money for her sister's studies for interest. By committing that, she took money for interest and gave it to her mother.

Fate and luck already decided, to benefit Samara. When good opportunity comes, we have to think about our future and growth. Off course we have to take suggestions and guidelines. But never ever give chance to anyone to stop you. Select a right path, if you deserve you will achieve it.

There was a Beauty competition organized by some club. With prior permission from Samara's Father-in-law, Samara decided to participate in the competition. Samara gathered all the materials and artificial ornaments required. Samara herself stitched her dress for the competition. Yes!, Samara was also one among the 25 Participants, she received an award for that.

Many noticed Samara, she got good opportunities. She received a proposal from one of the Film Director. The director sent his assistants and some team members to her home to discuss with Samara's father-in-law.

Greedy people who are with us they try to stop, harm and pull us back, It was Samara's father-in-law's wife. She took major part in spoiling Samara's life. This time she put a strong poison in her husband's mind.

It was evening time, Father-in-law called Samara. Granny, mother-in-law, Father-in-law and his son and daughter all were sitting in a hall. Samara's father-in-law asked Samara, "Why did you send people to me to ask/permit you to act in film". Samara was not knowing who had come and what they had asked. Innocently, she replied to Father-in-law, "I didn't send any one to you". Father-in-law in a aggressive manner, "No!, you wanted to change your profession to acting, you want to be an Actor, that's why you sent people to propose me". Samara's reply was "No!, I don't have any knowledge about this, No one proposed me." Mother-in-law in jealous, "Without your knowledge, how they can come here for discussion, you have planned everything and you are standing here like you don't know anything." Samara sat in front of her Granny with tears, "No Amma, I didn't, I don't even know the name of those people." Samara's eyes were bursting with tears. Granny can read her eyes she said, "Why unnecessary discussion." Granny directed her fingers towards her son angrily, "Its you, she took your permission and participated in the competition. Normally all the winners will be proposed by good director to act in their next project." You also know that.

Then Granny advised to Samara, "Look, this is not suitable for our family, as there are many girls in our family, this profession may not bring good husband for other girls in our family, Society will talk like anything. Again Samara's reply, "It was not me, I don't know who those people are."

Next day morning, Samara, was on her way to office, A friend wishes Samara, "Hi, How are you, I heard a news that you got a proposal from a director." Samara was shocked!. 'Except her many were knowing that she got a proposal from a director'. She asked her friend "How come you know?." He said the name of the person. Yes!, Samara knew him very well and she directly went to his office and asked him "Without my knowledge, why did you contacted my father-in-law?." Freind replied, "Oh Samara, calm down, I know unless your Father-in-law's permission you will not do anything, your decision depends on your Father-in-law's opinion. I know your nature from childhood." Samara in upset, "But it was not correct, it builds misunderstanding in our family and I am not interested in this and further please avoid contacting our family for the same reason".

Samara left the place and reached her office. When she reached the office there was also the same news. Person, who was the head of the department advised Samara, "Take it as my advice, **Good opportunities will not knock your door again and again, when it comes to you, you must accept and work for it.**"

Samara continued, "Decisions are not in my hand, Granny is taking care of me and I am under my father-in-law's shelter. Education and current position is a gift, remaining part of my life also I want to take his advice." Head of her office told, "Its all your choice, its up to you".

 Once person becomes famous, many eyes will be on them. People will notice, observe, like, criticize and express their opinion. Marriage is the beginning of other half part of life. Where everyone need and expect beautiful, smart partner in their life. But, It's between two families who shows interest and who accept it after several talk, demand and discussion. Everyone will not blessed as they wish, by luck only they marry whom they like. But fate knows when what should happen.

One of Samara's colleague proposed that he wanted to marry her. She was blank, "Oh God!, what is happening". She came and stood in front of him and said, "Please, I am not interested in marriage." He replied, "But my brother has already reached your home to talk about this with your family." She was shocked and sat on a chair and she said herself, "I am gone".

She took permission from her office and in a hurried manner came to her home, She asked Granny, "Amma has anybody come here." Granny questioned "No, Why?. "Amma I am just asking". She replied. Samara sat on the bench and took a long breath. There was a phone call, mother-in-law attended the call, other side of the phone the caller person asked "Is Samara available now?". Mother-in-law called Samara, "Samara, there is a call for you" and mother-in-law sat next to telephone table. Then Samara attended the call, She asked "Hello, who is this." Then the caller introduced herself and she is fifty years old lady, Samara knew her, the lady used to come to Samara's office, over the phone, lady said, "One of my brother, who is settled in the main city and he is a politician, wanted to marry you and your family need not required to spend anything for marriage, all he wants is you and opinion of your family. He is well settled, he has his own house, cars, money and servants. Please talk to your parents or put them on a call, I will talk to them and we can exchange kundali (Horoscope)." Samara was speechless simply holding the phone. The voice of the lady was clear and audible to Samara's mother-in-law, who was sitting next to the table. The lady over the phone asked Samara "Am I audible to you? , will you please talk to your parents and get back to me." Samara confusingly replied, "Yes, I will get back to you." Samara disconnected the call. Samara looking at her mother-in-law, she noticed that she heard everything. Samara rushed to her room. In Samara's room, Granny asked Samara, "Who was on call?, Whom were you talking for so long?. Samara nervously, "Ammaaa, that is,,, I know,, a lady, she used to come to our office.", Granny asked "But why did she call? , What is the matter?." Samara was nervous, Granny sat next to Samara holding her hand and asked "What is that? Why are you nervous, is there any problem." Samara nervously, "That,, That is,, she got a marriage proposal for me." She said, "The Gentlemen is a rich politician and he is interested in marrying me." She said, "He will bear all the expenses of the marriage, all he wants is yours and Father-in-law's opinion." Granny was excited and very happy, She said, "It is a very good news, let me talk to my son, let him come home." Granny was waiting for her son, he arrived home late, Granny decided to take it further, in next day morning.

In the next morning, Samara was sitting on her chair in the office, she got many rich and good marriage proposals but she was not in a position to accept it.

Dear readers, **"Always remember who ever you may be, if you get good opportunities, please select and accept it. Because your reaction may disappoint you in**

your future and you may regret for rejecting or you may not get good opportunities".

In the evening, Samara was in her room, Granny and her son were watching Television, mother-in-law was in other room. Granny was talking with her son, "See Samara has grown up and we have to find best match for her, as we know many relatives see and check in our relation." Son continued by saying, "We will search some other from outside of our relations". Granny was expecting the same answer, she took a chance and started telling, "In that case, Samara received a call from a lady, who was coming to her office, lady was telling that, her brother wants to marry Samara, the person is well settled politician, he needs our opinion and blessings, he will bear all the expenses of marriage". Son expressing his opinion, "Let us see, all of a sudden we can't take any decision, let us wait for some time". Granny while showing her interest, "We may not get such a good proposal, let us see and let us talk to them, we will see the kundali (Horoscope) and we will match it".

Next day morning, while having his breakfast, his wife started talking, "See you did a lot to Samara, now she has a job, name and everything, In future also she may get a good proposal, please stop worrying about her, you too have two daughters, why can't we propose that person to marry our elder daughter". Samara and

Granny heard this conversation. Granny came and asked her daughter-in-law, "Why are you so greedy, everything is decided by God, we should eat what is in our plate". Let us see her kundali (Horoscope), if it's matching then it is okay, otherwise we leave it".

 Samara's father-in-law asked Granny for Samara's kundali (Horoscope) and Granny went inside and she took the kundali (Horoscope) and stood in front of the god and requesting God, "Please bless God".

Ancestors were looking at that telling "Look at that we have a celebration, Samara got a proposal". Other one said, "It will not happen, backstabbing people will not leave her, they will spoil her life".

Granny gave that kundali (Horoscope) to her son. Granny was happy, she came to Samara's room and said "Everything I remember , you are blessed by Angels and ancestors, you will be happy in your life forever". Samara said, "Amma, Thank you, It's all because of your love and care, Thank you very much, for giving everything for me".

Next day evening, Granny and her son were talking about the kundali (Horoscope) , Son was telling to Granny "This is not right time for marriage and also she is having some dosha in her kundali (Horoscope) , she will not be happy in her life". Granny was broken, She raised a question, "No!, who said this to you?, you are completely wrong, long before, I had contacted person who wrote this kundali (Horoscope), he said it's wonderful, there are many opportunities and her father will be rich". Son interrupted and raised a question in laughter. "Where he is rich?". Granny became angered, she is explaining, "After her birth only you got promotion in your office, her arrival made you to construct home, you have received one good position and respect in your life". He again laughed at her and replied, "It is all because of my efforts".

Samara's father-in-law was Samara's God father and she respects him and his words, but she was crying.

Granny came and told to Samara, "Don't worry everything will be alright". Granny took her to astrologer's home, there was a long waiting line.

Granny greeted astrologer and she told to astrologer, "Your father wrote this kundali (Horoscope), please read this for us". Astrologer was an experienced person, he saw the kundali (Horoscope) and asked her, "Tell me what do you want to know about?". Granny asked, "Please check Her Marriage and future". Astrologer said, "It's a right time, you can proceed".

Granny asked "Is there any dosh in this kundali (Horoscope)". He is convincing Granny, "Every kundali (Horoscope) is having any one dosh and also has solution for that. You have to follow certain steps, do regular Pooja. Things will be alright". Granny doubted and said, "Don't feel bad my son said Samara will not be happy in her life". Astrologer was quite for some time and said, "We are not God, no one can decide anybody's life, kundali (Horoscope) shows our fate. It depends on our past karmas. No one will lead a happy life in their whole life, everyone will face the problem as per their karma, sometimes because of our best practice, pooja and meditation in present life, people will receive good luck. However, evil eyes and bad surroundings will spoil happiness, not our fate. Our own people, best friends, will not like our growth."

 "There are many good lucks and achievements in this kundali (Horoscope), please don't worry, If you have a good marriage you can proceed and don't wait for next year. In coming year Grahagati (Planetary positions) will be changed."

 Some how Granny was happy. She was telling Samara, "Don't worry, everything will be alright".

Things became normal, all marriage proposals were kept aside. Samara changed her plan.

 One day, Samara telling to her Granny, "Amma, in our office, one of our officer said that there is a good opportunity to the graduates. Government is motivating and providing loans to start their own small scale business. They give subsidy also". Granny raised a question, "Why business and risk?, marry a good person and be happy with your family. Samara answered, "I don't want to marry anyone". Granny convincing her, "Many obstacles comes in life, you have to accept it and move. You should not speak like that you are not interested in marriage". Samara requesting, "Amma, Please, please let me try this". Granny told, "Okay, you take permission from your father-in-law". Samara was happy, she expressed, "Thank you Amma".

Next day morning, Samara explained her father-in-law, she detailed about the loan provided by Government, documents required, subsidy and process. He permitted "Okay, go ahead".

Samara gathered all the documents and applied for loan. Samara attended the interview, after she completed her training, finally her loan was approved, she has to submit some additional documents. Address and agreement copy of the building, where she is starting her own shop.

Dear readers, "In life, many face different problems and failure. No one will become rich with one plan and approach. Yes!, If with proper support from family and friends and with the required investment, there is a chance of success. Without investment, no one can start a business. Samara took her father's help for the first time in her life".

Samara visited her father's native, She asked her father for a loan of Rupees Twenty Thousand for investment, he said that he doesn't have that much but he will ask with some people for interest. He arranged the loan for 10% Interest. This is another fall in Samara's life.

Samara came back to Granny's home and paid the amount as a advance (Security Deposit) to the owner of the shop. She signed the agreement.

She submitted, copy of the building rental agreement to the Bank Manager.

Samara asked the Bank Manager, "How many days of time will it take for the process and sanction". The bank Manager replied, "You have already attended the training and interview, your loan application was already selected, we were waiting for building rental agreement. Now everything is clear as you have given all the required documents, hardly it takes a week." Samara was so happy and she happily said, "Thank you sir!".

As Samara did not resign from her job, she was going to the office, she was sitting on a chair, she was thinking, "I have taken a loan for interest from my father, soon after receiving the loan from the bank, I have to clear this. I have to work hard to achieve success".

But not everything is in our hand. Two weeks gone, there was no update from the bank, She thought to visit the bank. One fine day, she went and met the bank manager and she greeted, "Hello sir, how are you doing?". The manager replied, "Yes Samara, I am doing good, how are you doing?, Please take your seat." Samara while sitting, "Yeah, good , I just wanted to know the status of the loan application that I have applied for". Manager replied, "Some days ago, I have informed your father-in-law that your loan has been sanctioned, but your father-in-law said not to inform you". Samara asked "But why sir". Manager replied, "I really don't know Samara". Samara thought to come back to home.

She told to Granny that loan she applied was sanctioned and Granny was happy, Samara called her Granny, "Amma". With full of tears. By looking at her eyes, Granny asked, "Why, Why are you crying?". Samara replied, "Long back loan was sanctioned, but father-in-law told to the bank manager not to process, not to inform me". Granny asked her, "Why will he tell like that".

It was evening, son came home, while having his coffee, Granny raised a question "Have you met the Bank manager regarding the Samara's loan, application, why did you tell him to stop the process? And why you did not inform about it to Samara".

Father-in-law called, "Samara". Samara came out from her room. She said "Yes, father in law". Her father-in-law told her, "Your loan was sanctioned, but there is a problem, my wife also wanted to run her shop, she didn't find a better place and shop for which you paid advance, if you give that place to her she will be happy.

Samara replied, "But I have submitted the rental agreement to the bank, after that only they sanctioned the loan, moreover now where I will search a new building, how will I submit the documents again, please understand". Father-in-law by selfishness, "I don't want any reason, you have to give that place to your Aunty, you search for a new shop".

Samara requested lot, "Please uncle, if I don't take loan in the given period, they will cancel it". Samara tried to convince him but she failed".

Granny was sitting and watching them both. She started talking, "Sorry to interrupt". She is telling to her son "Please tell me, have you completely gone mad and decided to destroy her life?". Before taking every step, Samara taken your permission. Are you playing with her emotions and life, First you will permit her and after everything you stop her, stop doing this, you constructed and messed her life.

Son raised his voice, "Where did I stop her?". Granny angrily, "Shut up. First in beauty competition you permitted and she earned a prize". It was not her fault, film director sent a proposal to you and you shouted at her".

"Second time, when Samara received a marriage proposal and when the person who was ready to marry her contacted us directly, you rejected".

"Now this, tell me one thing have you people decided to kill her or what, why you both are stopping her?. Leave your wife, what happened to you, why are you behaving like enemy to her?, Why are you jealous?, How you become so greedy?.

Granny by holding Samara's hand convincing her, "You go and start working, everything will be alright"

Son warning his mother, "Look if she wants to open a shop in same building let her leave this house and start her business, let her live separate, I don't want to see her face.

By hearing this Granny was speechless, just imagine when a person doesn't have any one except her Granny and Father-in-law. When Father-in-law says to leave the home and start your shop and live separately. Is it possible, Does anybody think that it can be done, what the society will tell? and what everyone will talk?. People will say her wings are grown, she needs freedom, she is regardless.

Months gone, Samara has to pay interest for the money she borrowed from her father, her father forced her, She again borrowed money for interest to pay her loan taken from her father.

Dear Readers, "In life never try to do something which is not reachable, If you got a proposal please accept, opportunity will not knock your door again and again. If you have a goal, and have a workable plan, Never take time, launch it and move forward, please stop worrying about others".

Time was melting, everything was out of Samara's hand, unless she receive loan from the bank, she can't open her shop, unless profit she can't clear the loan and interest was growing.

Please note all, **"Never spoil or damage anyone's life".** For the first time Father-in-law's daughter came and gave saffron(Tilak) to Samara. It was the beginning of the ending.

Samara was unable to do anything, she just decide to commit suicide, she went to temple close to a river. She thought of jumping in to that river and giving her life, since there was a huge crowd, she came back home. She took a handful of sleeping tablets and took a glass of water. Granny saw her doing that, before Granny tried to stop Samara, everything was over.

Granny by holding Samara's shoulder asks her, "What is this, what did you do, Oh God! What happened?". Samara became unconscious. But things were out of control.

Granny with full of fear and pain she is calling, "Samara!, Samara, please open your eyes!, Samara please talk to me!".

Dear Readers, "If you really care, like and love, after everything you facilitate and help them to grow. Don't spoil them if you don't like their growth. Because there is a payback for both good and bad deeds and now they are suffering for what they did to Samara".

This is not the end. Story will continue, I will come back, please take a break.

Dear readers, thank you for reading MY STORY.

**Yours
Samara
Saraswathi**